Breath of Joy

Poems,
Prayers,
and Prose

By
Danna Faulds

Danna Faulds

Peaceable Kingdom Books
Greenville, Virginia

ISBN 978-0-9744106-9-2

Author photo on back cover courtesy of
Marc Gordon.

Additional copies of this book, and all books by
Danna Faulds
are available by e-mailing the author at
yogapoems@aol.com

Printed in the U.S.A. by
Morris Publishing ®
3212 East Highway 30
Kearney, NE 68847
1-800-650-7888
www.morrispublishing.com

This book is dedicated to

Betty Davis-Drewery

Roberta Hamlin

Tora Huntington

Grace Welker

Wise women all, the four of you have graced my life with laughter, love, support, creativity, generosity, perspective, clear seeing, and the immeasurable gift of your friendship. I could not have made it through the last year without you! Heartfelt thanks and a deep bow of respect and admiration.

Other Books by Danna Faulds

Go In and In: Poems From the Heart of Yoga (2002)

One Soul: More Poems From the Heart of Yoga (2003)

Prayers to the Infinite: New Yoga Poems (2004)

From Root to Bloom: Yoga Poems and Other Writings (2006)

Limitless: New Poems and Other Writings (2009)

Into the Heart of Yoga: One Woman's Journey: A Memoir (2011)

Danna's poetry also appears in:

Sayings of Swami Kripalu: Inspiring Quotes From a Contemporary Yoga Master, edited with introduction and commentary by Richard Faulds.

Swimming with Krishna: Teaching Stories from the Kripalu Yoga Tradition, edited with commentary by Richard Faulds.

The Enlightenment Teachings of Yogeshwar Muni, American Disciple of Swami Kripalu, edited by Richard Faulds.

All books are available by e-mailing Danna at yogapoems@aol.com. Wholesale prices are available for purchases of five books or more.

Introduction

Joy. This introduction is all about joy, and I've resisted writing it for months. Then one morning, unable to sleep, I meditated for a bit, picked up a pen, and wrote:

> This is what I have to say to you. You have something to say about joy — something you have spent a lifetime learning. What exactly are you waiting for? You don't have to be finished or enlightened. Just write what you know to be true, to the best of your ability, but do it NOW...

As soon as I read what I'd written, I knew it was true. It was time to share what I'd learned. But joy has always been a charged subject for me. As a small child, being joyful led me to being called on the carpet as "too big for my britches," one of my mother's favorite phrases.

What did that mean, really, *"too big for my britches?"* The message I internalized was that being a strongly expressed little girl in touch with something vital and alive within me was risky business. Since giving voice to joy was likely to result in getting yelled at, I put a lid on my capacity to let life fill me with elation. I chose to fill tiny britches with just the iceberg's tip of the energy I was capable of experiencing.

Fast-forward more than fifty years to a November morning in 2011, when I went out on our deck as usual to put seed in the bird feeder and engage in an active breathing practice I have always loved. Known in Kripalu Yoga as Breath of Joy, it combines deep breathing with a fluid, easy motion of the arms.

Standing with my feet hip width apart, and knees slightly flexed, I inhale and raise my arms to shoulder height in front of me. Inhaling a little more, I sweep my arms out to the sides, again at shoulder height. Inhaling even more, my lungs fill completely as I raise my arms overhead, palms facing each other.

Swinging my arms toward the ground, I exhale with a breathy "ha" sound. As I bend forward from the hips, the momentum of the movement carries my arms behind me. As I bring my torso back up, I start to inhale, and move right into the next round.

While practicing Breath of Joy, I feel like Leonard Bernstein conducting the symphony of morning and the concerto of the yard. I breathe life in, just as it is in that moment, then let it all go in a full exhalation. After doing the practice every morning for years, one day it sparked this poem:

Breath of Joy

After the feeder is full
and seed is scattered
on the deck, I practice
Breath of Joy. It is a
moment of union with
weather and seasons.
I commune with
the moon if it's still
visible, with mist
or rain if it is falling.
If the sun is up, I lift
my face to catch its rays.
For ten rounds of breath,
I am one with earth
and sky before returning
inside, much to the glee
of the chickadees,
who are on the feeder
before the door can
close behind me.

The poem itself is far from noteworthy and would normally have been relegated to the "For My Eyes Only" pile. But that morning and every morning since, it has brought a simple ritual more fully into my conscious awareness. Breath of Joy brings me present, connects me to the air I breathe, the sky above me, and the earth beneath. It often leaves me smiling because it is exhilarating to move my body, fill and empty my lungs, and stand my ground no matter what the weather.

It's amazing to witness myself shifting from doubt, self-judgment, low energy, or despair, just by flapping my arms and breathing deeply. Often, in the course of ten rounds of Breath of Joy, my defenses drop and I experience a moment of wholeness and joy. This is no small thing for me, as one who has wrestled with depression and moodiness much of my life. Joy? It seems positively subversive and taboo to admit that I begin many mornings in a state of quiet joy.

As soon as I penned the poem, I knew that "Breath of Joy" would be the title of my next poetry book. What I didn't know was that the poem would launch me on an inquiry into the nature of joy that has lasted nearly two years and continues to be deeply enriching. What have I found? The most radical discovery is that joy is everywhere when I open up and look closely. That astounds me.

Joy is often seen as the mind state that results from the occurrence of something positive. I get the job I want or leave the job I hate, and experience an inner burst of joy. Webster's defines joy as "the emotion evoked by well-being, success, or good fortune, or by the prospect of possessing what one desires." Contrary to Mr. Webster, my experience is conclusive and unequivocal. If I have the presence of mind to look for joy, or ask if joy is there, it always is. Even in the midst of a migraine, or right in the middle of fear or self-doubt.

What I am talking about here is joy for no reason, a joy that is innate and natural. While joy may not lend itself to easy definition, I immediately recognize when it wells up inside me—that sense of elation, optimism, and present-tense knowing that all is truly well. When joy is flowing through me, I feel a sense of infinite optimism. Energy moves upward, spilling out of me and into the world like a fountain sending spray in all directions.

Joy connects what once felt separate. It bridges chasms of doubt and contains within it the knowing that something far bigger than my small mind or fortunate circumstance is the source of all that is wondrous in life. Joy has within it great strength and great vulnerability.

If I had to offer my own definition, I would say that joy is the movement of divinity within. It is the ecstasy of existence. Ecstasy not because everything is perfect, or the way I want or expect it to be, but because everything is as it is, and I am not separate from that "isness." Joy as the ecstasy of existence is not a mind state, but something that bubbles up continuously from the source of All That Is. My ability to experience, tap into, and relish its miraculous existence rises and falls, but joy itself is ever-present.

Over the years that I've been inquiring into the experience of joy, several practices have come to me that enhance my ability to contact joy. The active breathing practice I often do on my deck was the first of those practices. When I let myself really get into the moving, breathing flow of that exercise, it kindles a hidden spark of inner joy. As a result, I've practiced Breath of Joy almost every morning, rain or shine, in temperatures below zero and when it's already 80 degrees with the sun just over the horizon. I can be grouchy as all get out, but if I can make myself move my arms and breathe, I find myself feeling lighter, more free, and in touch with the joy of being alive.

A different and more meditative practice has also been potent, one that involves breathing in joy and breathing out anything that blocks me from joy. When I do this, breathing out distraction, resistance, fatigue, whatever seems to get in the way of joy flowing freely, eventually the joy I breathe in fills me to overflowing and there is nothing to do but breathe joy in and breathe joy out. This perfect circle of joy—inbreath connected to outbreath, connected to inbreath—is indescribably precious. The fact that I can offer joy into the world from the depth of my being feels like nothing short of a miracle to me.

Another practice I've used to bring me to a heightened awareness of joy is asking the question "What's true here" in my meditation. I ask it when I'm lost in spinning thoughts or dark emotions. Instead of avoiding those thoughts and feelings, I let the question drill down through layer after layer, feeling and experiencing each one until I hit bedrock. And the bedrock always occurs to me as joyous.

During meditation, I've also focused my awareness on what I think of as the interface between form and formless, a place inside that isn't a point exactly, but more of a continuum, where it seems that I can directly experience the world coming into being. I find it by being very attentive to that subtle emanation of divinity within. My experience is that the formless comes into form through a flow of energy, and it is the contact with that energy that lets me know I'm "there." When I can sit with that sense of flow for even a short time, I find myself uplifted and joyous. Where my small-self can be dissatisfied, uncomfortable, or even angry, the vast me, the impersonal me is consistently joyous beyond belief.

I shake my head in wonder as I write this because joy seemed so very out of reach for me not that far back. After my father's death in 2010, I was so identified with my despair and hopelessness that it felt like all of me, permanent, forever, with a "no exit" quality that was horrifying. The story of how I moved from being stuck in anxiety, depression, and angst to where I am today is longer than I can tell here, but it includes the practices I've just described. Somehow, slowly, and not in any linear fashion at all, I moved through the stuck places back into the flow.

This book came into being as I made that journey back to joy. And while I am not, by any stretch of the imagination, always in a joyous state, I've come far enough to know that if I remember to ask if joy is here, the answer is always a resounding "Yes." That yes might turn back into a scowl a moment later, but string together enough moments of joy and it begins to transform everything, healing what needs to be healed and creating me anew each day.

That's where I am right now, stringing those joyous moments together as I witness my own re-creation. Sometimes connected, sometimes out of touch, I am always grateful for the practices that brought me here, the people who helped me along the way, and the presence of divinity and joy.

11

Joy is inherently creative, and the practices I've described here are what organically arose over time from my daily explorations of yoga, meditation, and life. The real question, the more important question, is what connects *you* to joy? What are the particular practices and pursuits that light your inner spark and allow you to feel the ecstasy of existence?

Positive psychologist and Kripalu teacher Maria Sirois says: "When you have the choice, which you do in every moment of every day, lean toward joy." I think that's great advice. Who cares if I leaned in the other direction for decades? What matters is that I'm here right now, exploring joy, giving myself over to it, letting it dance inside my heart and flow out into the world through the simple act of being unashamedly alive.

What follows is a selection of poems, prayers, and prose written since 2008, inspired by my journey. Thank you for your interest and support. They mean more to me than I can say.

Danna Spitzform Faulds
October, 2013

Consider the Lilies

Consider the lilies,
how they use their
precious blooming to
share beauty with
this world. You, too,
were born to open
in the light. You, too,
are given life to
cultivate your gifts
and let them lift you
out of fear and doubt.
A vast garden of love
is all around you now
if you can see beyond
the tangled weeds
to the mystery and
radiance beneath.

Recipe

Take one precious
human life. Add a
slice of mindfulness,
a heaping cup of
contemplative practice –
any flavor you choose.
Dissolve the personal
self in a quart of self-
inquiry. Blend laughter,
love, well-being, prayer,
awareness, ease, and truth.
Mix ingredients and bake
until done. Recipe serves
everyone. Leftovers can
be used in open-faced,
non-dual sandwiches.
Feel free to experiment
with unusual ingredients.
Cooking time will vary.

Prayer Lessons

I ask the trees to teach me
how to pray and, being innately
generous, of course they oblige.
The old trees seem most
knowledgeable, but even the
saplings lift their limbs to the
sky without ceasing. The trees
speak to me of silence and
patiently waiting for answers.
They describe how to recognize
divine presence in dirt,
in biting winds, and pristine
starry nights. Prayer is no
different than life, they tell me,
sometimes difficult, always
an act of faith. One black walnut
raises his voice above the rest.
"Follow the example of the
goldfinch," he says. "Goldfinches
pray while they eat, pray as
they fly, pray whether their
feathers are bright yellow or
dull green. I've never seen a
goldfinch who isn't glad to be
alive, and grateful for the
least little twig to land on."

Breathe In, Breathe Out

Breathe in spaciousness and
acceptance of what is.
Breathe out resistance.
Breath in possibility and
optimism. Breathe out fear
and doubt. Breathe in ease.
Breathe out the need
to change the way
this moment is unfolding.
Breathe in the certainty
that what we really are is
so much bigger than pain
and suffering. Breath out
limitation and conditioning.
Breathe in divinity and
openness. Breathe out a
prayer of thanks that even
in the midst of difficulty,
there is awareness.

What If I Knock?

What if I knock
and nothing happens?
What if I knock
only to have the
door slammed soundly
in my face? What if
I decide to wait until
I feel courageous and
worthy, and that day
never comes? What if
I knock and the
door opens? What if
I'm invited inside,
welcomed, embraced,
no trace of judgment
anywhere? What will
I say? What if the
biblical promise is real
and every knock—
no matter how timid
or bold—opens a door
whether I know it or not?
What if the door has
been open the whole
time, while I dithered
and doubted at the
threshold, while I
waited and paced?
What if I lived from
the premise that I'm
already inside?

Wholeheartedly

I'm not giving up,
even though I don't
know how to go
forward, how to hoist
myself out of this hole
and not fall right
back in. I don't know
anything, really,
but isn't that the
only place to start –
a clean slate,
the launch pad with
a rocket waiting
for lift off?
The countdown is
ticking off the
final seconds and
there is no excuse
in the world now
to hold back from
the wild and
unpredictable ride
this life will be if
I throw myself into
it wholeheartedly.

Ministry of Words

Mine is a ministry of words.
My pulpit is the page,
my bread and wine the
inspiration that guides mind
and hand to write. I rarely
see my congregation face-
to-face, but I feel you
with me nonetheless,
listening, whispering
encouragement. We're all
in it together, this holy church
of life. When the collection
plate is passed, let's give
generously, offering our
willingness to be seen
as we really are, offering
our creativity and desperation,
our questions, prayers,
and fears. May each moment
be a revelation, our lives more
calling than career. And may
the benediction of wonder
descend upon us and rise up
from inside so we stay awake
for the sermon that speaks—
that always speaks—from the
very heart and center of the soul.
                    Amen!

I Do

Wild rhododendron climb the hillsides
and reach down the steep banks
toward the creek. With such a short
season, it's a privilege to see these blooms,
pink in bud, white in open blossom.

Like bridal bouquets, the flower clusters
line the trail, marrying the green of
growing things with blue sky and the
black wings of flying crows.

Do you take this beauty into your heart,
to love and cherish 'til death do you part?
"I do," trills the indigo bunting, a flash of
azure disappearing in the brush.
"I do," says the lizard, sunning on a rock.

I hear my own true voice speak up,
the voice that comes not from mind or
thought but from the center of the great
silence where all beauty has its root.

"I do." The words reverberate clear
through me and transform a bike ride
I've done a hundred times into a shining
moment tinged with wonder.

I take nature as my sacred partner,
leaving separation far behind - all by the
grace of the rhododendron blooms.

Remind Me

Lord, let me carry the lamp
of your love into my day.
Remind me that nothing can
extinguish that flame – not rain,
not wind, not the busy fray of
the marketplace. Remind me
of its light when my mind
spins in tight circles and
I forget my divine source.
Remind me again and again
of the love that sent me forth.

This is what I have to say to you. If you feel joyful, do not hesitate to express that truth. If you feel anxious, do not turn away or try to run from that experience. If you feel both at once, hold the paradox with open hands and do not force either to be your only reality.

Move toward your direct experience of life and make no excuses. If you are messy, be messy. If you are clear, let clarity pour out far and near. If you are both at once, span the distance that is really no distance at all, but two sides of the same thin line, two aspects of humanity, two ways to move back through communion into oneness. There is nothing to fear here, not even your own death, that moment when you slip back into what you've always been.

Without Darkness

Be the cup that holds
the candle. Be the wax,
the wick, the flip of the
wrist that lights the match.
Most of all, be the flame.

Draw on the source
of light, acknowledging
that without darkness,
candles would be
useless things indeed.

From the Beaks
Of Wise Ones

Crow call sounds
for all the world
like "Now! Now! Now!"
I try to bring my mind
back from distant
wanderings.

A second crow offers a
different refrain. "Stay awake!
Stay awake! Stay awake!"
Having received these
messages from the beaks
of wise ones, I do my
utmost to comply.

Resolution

Whereas it is the very nature
of the mind to compare,
label, draw distinctions,
and see separation where
none exists; and whereas
truth is unified and will
not be changed by any
machinations of a
problem-solving mind;
whereas human and
divine are not two,
but one, and that one
is alive inside me; be it
hereby resolved that
I will not be tempted
into thinking I am less
than the infinite clothed
in skin, All That Is
seeing itself from my
unique perspective and
then dropping all views
to be freedom itself.
To this solemn and
celebratory resolution
I set my hand and
seal, releasing myself
from the need to do
anything in particular,
while knowing with
certainty that the
universe will act
through me for the
greatest good when I
choose to let it do so.

Your Grace

Lord, the power of our dialogue
is slowly coming clear.
You speak, and I grow quiet
to receive your guidance.
I pray, and you take in
my prayers. Either way,
we draw near, the barriers
between us disappearing.

It doesn't matter what
language I speak, what name
I cry out when my longing
leads me into your embrace.
It doesn't matter if I feel
inarticulate or become
distracted in mid-prayer.

What's important is that I
keep coming back into
relationship, back into
spaciousness, vulnerability,
and awe. When I do this,
your presence frames
the way I look at life and
your grace pervades even
the most difficult of days.

Always Home

I am a ship tied
to this dock by the
flimsiest of ropes.
A good, strong gust
of wind – and I'm
free, the polished
timbers of my hull
slipping through the
water with such ease.

The far mountains in
the twilight are
bewitching – and I
might go there,
though the open sea
calls too. Instead of
plotting a course,
navigating my way
to a chosen destination,
I surrender to the
currents and the waves.

My sails are full and
the one thing I'm sure of
is that letting go will
bring the best result.
Maps and plans are like
so much spray from
breaking waves,
while allowing the
journey to unfold in
its own wild way
will always bring
me home.

Love Generators

Love is alive,
each one of us
the bull's eye
on love's target.
Pierced to the very
center and source
by the generous
energy of love,
there is no other
course but to
become love
generators, little
dynamos radiating
the truth of love
in all its infinite
disguises.

My Calling

Between the two poles
of faith and doubt,
my life arcs like
a rainbow. Between the
extremes of aversion
and greed, I stretch,
a taught string, rarely
relaxing. Between the
two ends of surrender
and willful action,
my practice unfolds,
always a surprise to me.
I know the truth of
the Absolute and the
beauty of the relative.

My calling in this life
is to grow so wide that
form and formless are
unified inside me,
creative energy pouring
forth in poems and other
bold expressions of
the whole. I am the bridge
between visible and
invisible, so at home
with paradox that I cease
pointing in one direction
or the other and enter
fully the unknown
of this moment.

Practice

Practice for the sheer joy
of being free. Practice
to be empty of "me, me, me."
Silent, open, and infinitely vast,
practice to remember what is real.

Practice to give yourself up
and receive the wordless truth.
What you get will be useless –
not the coin of any realm –
but oh, the glory of
those moments—being whole.

Source of All Healing

May the source of
all healing fill me
with light, illuminating
even the dark corners
of body and mind.

May the truth beyond
the physical shine through,
reminding me that I am
more than flesh or fear.

May universal energy
fuel my life so surrender
and truth can both
be realized, the two paired,
like breath and air,
to strip me of illusions.

This is what I have to say to you. You long for wonder when wonder is all around you. You long for freedom, and freedom is the very foundation upon which your world is built. You long for creativity, which never stops flowing into you. You long for a direct experience of truth, and that's what you are—you can't escape your true nature even if you wanted. You long to be awake, and that is a choice you can make, moment by moment. When you forget to make it this breath, choose it in the next. You long to be one with the divine, and that is your radiant essence. You long to break free of conditioning, yet you let yourself spin endlessly in the same worn grooves of thought.

Any time you choose, you can leap out of these ruts and receive with gladness the day as it is arrayed before you. Let longing transform itself into gratitude and yearning morph into love. Whatever you wish for, find it now, celebrate it here, experience it fully before you forget again what's real.

Communion

A single spent sunflower
bows its heavy head
over the garden.
Chickadees balance on
big leaves and pluck
the seeds, one by one,
to crack and eat.
Their communion needs
no prayer but wind
and sun, each seed the
perfect body of the One.

The Word

In the beginning
was the word,
and the word
called all of us
into being.
The word whispered
"Come," and one
by one we slid
into this world
convinced we were
separate creatures,
believing life was
a series of hurdles
to jump, and failure
was the likely outcome.

The word was lost
to us, or maybe
we still heard it
dimly, but we didn't
pay it any heed.
Gradually we learned
to listen, or perhaps
the word shouted
loudly. Whatever
the route, one day
we knew again, and
the word drew us
back into its embrace.

Then the word
spoke through us,
saying what we
didn't know we knew,
and it kept speaking
without ceasing until
we could willingly,
joyfully, expansively
choose silence.

Love and the Great Silence

There is nothing fair or lovely
about life, although sometimes
it is both. Life is simply
what it is – unapologetically
bold in its approach. It can
bowl me over with beauty
or leave me flattened
by grief, and doesn't even
blink at my reaction.

If I curse the gods or fate,
my life is bound by anger
and regret. If I let the sadness
dissolve me completely,
love is all that's left –
love and the great silence
underlying every breath.

The Full Power of Joy

Distraction succumbs easily to joy.
Self-judgment falls next, and then
fear is flattened when joy
flashes past. I never knew, until now,
the full power of joy to recast
my psyche – and my life –
simply by bathing me in light.

The Key to My Heart

I didn't know it was
your door I was
knocking on.

I didn't know it
was your hand that
held the key
to my heart until
the secret was
unlocked and I stood
before you freer than
I'd ever been before.

I didn't know my
destiny and yours
were woven with
one thread,
the whole cloth
of our coming together
a mystery I cherish.

Gather Me In

Gather me in, Lord.
From my far-flung,
peripheral distractions,
draw me into the
center of your heart.
May the gravitational
tug of your love
and the silent promise
of your presence
eclipse the glitz and
glitter of this world.

May I find you in
the quiet places,
amidst the wildflowers,
inside the rising, falling
call of flying goldfinches.
No matter how far
I may have strayed,
gather me in to where
every breath partakes
of your essence and
makes it possible for me
to know the truth and
glory of this singular
and so commonplace
of moments.

Keeping the Sabbath

On the seventh day
we rested and gave thanks.
The crows bowed low
to the sun as it rose
and the wrens sang
in praise to the creator.
Even the rocks rested.

On the seventh day,
this wild experiment
that is life paused
for a moment to appreciate
the whole. Most of the
creatures showed their
gratitude in silence.

From deep woods
to open fields,
there was a palpable
sense of contentment
when expectations
slipped away and there
was nothing to do but
keep the Sabbath.

Oops

It was a brief snooze,
but there I was,
sawing psychic wood,
unconscious as could be.
What could I do but laugh
when I caught myself
believing what I don't believe,
so entangled in old patterns
that I could barely breathe?
Catnaps happen to the best
of us, you know, but I'm
awake now, awake and glad
and grateful for my eyes-
wide-open receptivity and
the ease of moving on.

The Act of Being

Don't look outside,
and don't look inside either.

Don't look up or down
or sideways.

Don't seek answers
where they cannot be found.

In the quiet, open spaces
of the heart, just be yourself

and let the act of being
lead you into now.

This is what I have to say to you. Because the divine is truly infinite, and because you are divine, this is a day of infinite possibility. You can choose to see it as a humdrum, so-so, hurdle of a day, an obstacle to skip over on your way to somewhere else. Or you can open to the beauty that is all around you, no matter your surroundings.

Until the moment of your death, there is always breath. There is always sky, sunlight, and the ever-changing sensations of the bodymind. Behind all this is the vast, undifferentiated matrix, the source of All That Is. Give yourself into it. Explore the immeasurable essence and emptiness of it. Lose yourself in its embrace. Take advantage of this day in big and small ways.

Caught in the Act

Halfway to breakfast,
a field of yellow flowers
overpowered my senses
and led me to forget the
berries and dried fruit
nestled in the bottom
of my picnic basket.

The promise of a future
feast pales in the face
of nature's immediacy,
the overflowing plenitude
of spring caught in
the act of awakening.

Surrender the Relative

Surrender the relative
into the Absolute,
love releasing into love.
Find what is changeless,
whole, and free,
and give the reins
of your life over
to that mystery.
Nothing is lost or
defeated when you
surrender to what's real.
It may feel like
losing yourself,
but you are actually
gaining the universe.

Awake

Awake to celebration,
awake to pain,
awake to the day
as it is, awake to
wishing the day
was different. Awake
to vastness and constriction,
awake to fear and ease
and suffering.
Awake to infinite silence,
awake to the confused
cacophony of the
conditioned mind.
Awake to seeking and
the end of seeking.
Letting it all in.
Letting it all be.
This is me.

Ground Note

If praise to the creator
forms the day's foundation,
how can the hours that follow
be anything but blessed?
Intoxicated by wild phlox,
I turn my eyes skyward.
Swallows and purple martins
sweep over the creek.
Much higher, an eagle glides
along the ridge top.
Tree frogs and stream
sounds blend with the
rustle of new leaves.
When gratitude is the
ground note, all discord
falls away.

Healing Happens

The unseen, unloved,
unconscious aspects of
my being let themselves
be glimpsed in dreams
and drive my behavior
from behind the scenes.
They rise into the light
only when the time
is right. Learning to
stay still and not react
when I am filled with
memories or moods
has been a challenge
and a choice. Slowly,
these inner knots are
letting go. Slowly,
old conditioning
dissolves to leave me
freer than before.
The mystery calls me
forward and healing
happens even when
I can't say for certain
what is healed.

What Debt Crisis?

What if the full faith
and credit of the universe
backed up my every move?

What if the interstellar
bank of cosmic energy
guarantees an endless flow
of creativity and grace?

What if my view of finite
resources isn't true,
and the cornucopia is
always spilling over
somewhere?

What if the only debt
we owe is to let our
immortal souls shine
freely, without fear of
foreclosure or bankruptcy?

The Light You Need

Hold the small self lightly
as the vast Self opens wide.
Abide in the whole truth
as the deathless, dancing
love song of the universe
plays through you.

In the end, it doesn't matter
if your moon is full or
waning; the light you need
to navigate even the darkest
night emanates freely
from inside.

True Prayer

I feel the subtle
summons to prayer,
that turn of the heart
toward the indescribably
wide horizon of the divine.

It is a yearning – yes –
but also a recognition
that what I yearn for
is shockingly present.

Any words I speak
with my mouth or
think in my innermost
being disappear into
a receptivity that I
could label full
or empty, with either
descriptor correct and also
woefully inadequate.

My gratitude and entreaties,
even my most sincere
confessions pale in
the face of true prayer –
silence receiving silence.

This is what I have to say to you. You are connected through the breath, connected by the very essence of your being, not because you believe or know, or practice, but because your soul is always plugged in, always whole. Without having to do anything in particular, you are the bridge between the infinite and this transient realm of form. Your connection isn't something you can win or lose, and while you must choose to be aware of it, the divine is there, inside and out, ever present, whether you feel it or not.

Step out of the shoes of unworthiness and run barefoot on the grass of your true nature. Unafraid, let the connection of your soul to All That Is heal any remaining sense of separation. When you reach the right spot—and you can trust yourself to know it—plant your two feet squarely on the earth and reach for the sky. Let the energy of the universe move through you, shape you in its own image, sculpt you for its greater purpose. When you breathe your arms down to your sides, you will walk back into the world a different being, consecrated to the mystery, and living a life of open-ended possibility.

Morning Glories

It's a lovely morning
for the glories, pink
petals opened wide.
Last night's rain slaked
their summer thirst,
and today they vibrate
with the bees that buzz
inside. Theirs is a
brief life—blooming
for a few quick hours
before they're gone—
but I don't see a
single flower begging
for reprieve. They hold
their trumpets high as if
they have all the time
in the world to offer
silent blessings
to the sky.

Threads of Light

I listen inside,
open to the divine,
pay close attention
to whatever I find.

From these simple
steps, my life
and writing
unwind like
threads of light.

Rolling from an
unseen spool,
these luminous
strands weave
themselves into
the tapestry of me.

Love Channel

The heartbeat of
this world is love.
It's an underlying
thrum, a barely
perceptible vibration
that runs through
every breath and
prayer, through every
caring act.

It's even where love
seems to be entirely
lacking, but how much
better for humanity
if we tune our dials
to the love channel,
all of us seeing,
hearing, expressing,
and manifesting love
in its infinite imaginings.

Where Inquiry and Knowing Meet

Acknowledge the body,
acknowledge the mind,
embrace the relative realm
with all the energy and
gusto you can find –
just don't stop there.
Behind, beneath, beyond
sensory experience and
identity is the silent
spacious yes of your
true nature. Now I'm
not saying that this
world isn't real,
but there's more to you
than what you think,
taste, see, or feel.
Choose the whole,
and not the part.
Choose the fire, not
the spark. Acknowledge
your heart, but identify
only with what's infinite
and free, and eventually
let even that fall away
to leave the open space
where inquiry and
knowing meet as equals.

Find the Kindness

Reach deep inside
to find the kindness
needed to forgive
yourself for all
your trespasses.

Break the cycle
of harsh mind to
offer understanding
and compassion to
your own small self.

This doesn't mean
ignoring faults –
embrace the whole
of you instead of
judging separate parts.

The Unassailable Certainty of Wonder

I can't help myself –
I always feel
hopeful at dawn.
Watching the world
choose light over
dark and waking
over sleep, I just
can't stay grouchy.
Of course, the night
sky has its delights too.
When Orion's broad
shoulders catch my eye
and it appears he's
striding into his life
with such sparkling
fearlessness, I want
to cheer him on.
Give me an O!
Give me an R!
Give me an I!
Give me another O!
Give me an N!
What you have is
the unassailable
certainty of wonder.
What you have is the
wide-eyed gaze of a
child looking up,
asking, "Do you think
I can touch those stars?

Nothing More to Give

Some of us breeze
through the birth canal,
easy as you please,
while for others,
it's a near-death
experience just
to get here.
But once we enter
this world, we're all
in the same
leaky boat.
We struggle to
stay afloat,
bailing, flailing,
learning to swim,
donning life jackets.
We try prayer or
existential despair,
but nothing changes
the basic insecurity
of life. It all boils
down to such a
simple truth:
we can commiserate
in our misery or offer
each other acceptance,
warmth, and love.
We have nothing more
to give than this.

Wordless Sermon

The sea breathes its way
inside me. The rough and
tumble rush of waves
is balanced by the
easy way the water
recedes – clear blue
disappearing into
blue. All my senses
are awake to the
impersonal magnificence
of nature. Even the need
to pray drops away
beside the ocean's
wordless sermon.

One Small Slice

I feel flat, as if my
four dimensions have
collapsed into one thin
line that winds through
dark times. I feel dense,
the neutron star of my
emotions spinning
aimlessly in space.
An ocean of sadness
floods me at high tide,
the detritus of my life
washed up on shore
for all to see. It's easy
to take these feelings
seriously, to believe
them to be all of me
instead of one small
slice of a rich and
evolving life. When I
choose to let them be,
when I am grateful
rather than grasping,
laughing instead of
gnashing my teeth,
when I allow life
to be as it is,
it's clear that feelings
are just feelings while
truth is always truth.

The Great Perfection

On the day you were born,
angels clapped their wings
and sang your praises.
On the day you die, you will
be received back into
infinite safety.

Between now and then,
in this mystery we call life,
how much easier to see it
as the Great Perfection
playing out. The sooner you
realize that you, too, are divine,
the more easily the universe
can flow through you unimpeded.

On this day of days, go forth
knowing there are no mistakes
in the whole of this creation.

This is what I have to say to you. What is true right now? When you are open and receptive, what is your direct experience of this moment? If you lay down your defenses, what remains? When you release your past conditioning and let go of your small self, what draws your awareness? Ask the questions and let the answers come. Let them fill you up as if you are a cup and life a pitcher, pouring freely.

Find the place within where mystery resides. Let the tide of truth wash over you and don't even try to stay upright. Where the relative world of form and action comes together with the infinite and Absolute, rest there. Feel the embrace of the seamless, undivided whole, and know that as your true nature. Be unafraid, even as the vastness expands beyond the reach or comprehension of the mind.

Whatever you find in this brief journey of inquiry and experience, take it in as holy. You are so much bigger than you seem.

Locus of All Possibilities

There is a single point,
infinitesimally small,
yet wide as all creation,
where the personal lets go
into the void and the
impersonal rushes like a
flash flood into the
world of form.

We humans live at
this juncture, the locus
of all possibilities
at the center of our being.
Sit with it for a time,
and the potent mix of
nothing and everything
obliterates the mind.

Calla Lily

Georgia O'Keefe would
surely paint this single
petal curving round the
stamen, stark white
goblet held aloft to catch
the dew. I sit in quiet
admiration until I, too, spiral
into the center of its beauty
where life force pours
from foliage and bloom.
Every sense awake and
concentrated, the only view
is up, the only sight is
sky, the flower and I both
flowing out of silence.

The Stew of Life

Present to excitement and anxiety.
Present to body, mind, breath,
and the deathless essence shining
inside me. Present to the infinite
reach and particular needs of
this being. Present to the bubble of
joy, rising to the surface with a smile.
Present to the voices of doom, gloom,
and invincible optimism. Present to
resistance and acceptance.
Present with crows, doves, cardinals,
and love. Present to the stew of life,
whether plain or spiced, always
        a delectable surprise.

Womankind

Earth energy, feminine and
strong, rises up from my feet
to pull my spine long.
Earth blood courses through
me like mighty rivers
leaping over falls and small
streams singing as they
tumble to the sea.

I am womankind, with all
her fertile minds and wombs,
lullabies, looms, and blooming
gardens. Earth voice speaks
to me: "Do not forget that
you are the intersection
of human and divine.

You, my cherished sister,
exist as the open field
of every possibility because
my creative juices
flow within you.

Arise now and go forth,
undaunted by the road that
lies before you. Step into
this unknown bearing the gift
of your femininity and living
into the Infinite even as I
daily embrace both
night and sunrise."

Ode to a Silent God

I would like you to speak,
but you adorn the morning
with your silence. One by
one, I place my doubts at
your feet where they seem
to disappear. "At your feet,"
is just a figure of speech.
I cannot picture you
in a body. In fact, I have
no name for you, though I've
tried hard to find one.
I surrender body, mind,
and heart, and then I give
my needs into the open space
of your incorporeal embrace.
Whatever I give you ceases
to be mine, and this is,
I think, a priceless gift.

I'd like to paint your portrait,
but within the ornate frame
there would be nothing but
light, and sometimes not
even that. A frame is too
confining, of course. Imagine
All That Is squeezed inside
four slim pieces of wood.

When I offer you my fear,
it is no longer here, but lifted
like a great weight off my chest.
Anxiety rises like a wave that
threatens to break me in a
million little pieces. I sit

with it, and something in me
witnesses without being sucked
into anxiety's warped reality.
Eventually I remember to
give you this distress, which
noticeably lessens, but still
nibbles at the edges of my psyche.

I feel so vulnerable,
so out of control, but also
washed clean and thoroughly
seen, as if I am entirely transparent.
I'd still like you to speak, but the
silence is so natural and easy.
Now that my breath and yours
are indistinguishable, words
might be intrusive. So I bow
to you in gratitude, and give
you my practice of surrender,
to do with what you will.

Sweet Time

Great nature takes
her own sweet time.
No one can hurry
sunrise; migrating birds
arrive when they arrive;
trees grow and leaf
on their own unique
schedules. We are
the only creatures
with clocks, minute
hands marching in
tight circles, seconds
flashing past. Think of
the inner peace
if we awoke one day
to find that all the
clocks had turned into
flower pots filled with
buds that bloomed only
when a power greater
than calendars or hours
coaxed their petals open.

Opportunity to Trust

Remind me today to look
up as well as down,
in as well as out.

Remind me that doubt
and faith can coexist,
that anxiety doesn't
have to twist me into
knots I can't untie.

Remind me that
everything in my life
is infused with truth,
that the illusion of my
separateness won't
last once I see
through it.

Remind me that
this whole day is an
opportunity to trust
in unforeseen outcomes
and the ultimate
supremacy of love.

Prayer of the Five Senses

May your eyes see God
in all directions.

May your ears hear
harmony and dissonance
with equal pleasure.

May you feel the touch
of spirit, taste divine
nectar, smell the sweet
scent of the transcendent
and the real.

May every breath be
blessed with oneness,
and may you choose
to live in truth, giving
yourself fully to this
day's unfolding grace.

This is what I have to say to you. Into the open field of your awareness, into the circle of your life will come everything you need to make your way in this world. This isn't magic. It isn't something you have to make happen. Just open to receive, and the universe flows easily into the space that you've created.

Of course this takes faith. Of course it takes trusting yourself. Of course it may seem like nothing is happening, but in truth, what you need is coming forth from the infinite to meet you here in form. All you need to do is say yes. Again and again say yes. Push nothing away because true gifts come in surprising disguises.

Just a Dove

I lift my eyes up to the
red and rising sun, and feel
my heart lift with it.
The dark night is behind
me now. Light streams
through the trees and finds
a dove, midway between
feeder and pines. It glows
like the holy spirit,
wingtips lit, underside
shining as if the fire of the
Almighty is ignited in its
breast. When it comes to
rest in the shadows,
it is just a dove again,
although we both know better.

Shadows Aren't All of Me

Had I given in to my despair,
I would not be here bearing witness
to blue sky sharing space with clouds.
I would have never known that despair
melts into sadness, sadness into shame,
shame giving way to a nameless
emotion that dates back before
speech when I was powerless
and small and no one noticed
that I needed comfort.
Had I left my life before this day,
I never would have known that
darkness always shelters
something else. It took all these
years of practice to see that
shadows aren't all of me.

Listen and Receive

She is lovely, the wise woman
of my waking dream. The lines
of her face crinkle when she smiles
and her hands dance like butterflies.
She leans in close, her conspiratorial
whisper tickling my ear.

"Find your own way to the spirit,"
she says. "Let no man – or woman either –
decide how wide or deep your soul
can reach. Invite the sacred essence
at your core to come forth,
the round, receptive, realized one
who rejoices in the least of
God's creatures. She, whose creative
energies will lead her outside
the prison of her fear, is already here.
Listen," the wise woman tells me,
her clear eyes boring into mine.

"Every true path leads into the unknown,
and I am here to tell you there is
always a way forward." She repeats
the words for emphasis, "There is
always a way forward, and you will
find it if you dare to know yourself,
be yourself, believe in miracles,
and drink deeply of the grace that
showers down in every moment of
your day. I say, listen and receive."

Remembering and Unafraid

I pray to be the immovable truth
and the change that moves life forward.

When silence is my highest expression,
may I choose the quiet path;

When speech is needed,
may I communicate freely.

May I cut through the web of my neuroses,
with the boldness required to leave
conditioning behind.

In the fullness of time,
may I die into the presence and power
of what can neither be named nor tamed,
remembering, remembering,
remembering and unafraid.

Tantric Paradox

I am the inbreath, the outbreath,
and the pause between the two.

I am first light, sparrow flight,
the leading edge of morning
drawing me forward.

Sensations, thoughts, and dreams
are me, and the open space
in which these phenomena
seem so real until they disappear.

I am the yearning, burning urge
for truth and the whole truth,
ever-present, silent, wise, and
gleaming like a jewel at twilight.

I am all things and no thing,
the perfect tantric paradox
not boxing me into a philosophy,
but setting me free.

I'm the wings of creativity and
the flash of insight inviting me
outside my small self, inside the
vast and beckoning unknown.

It's Not About Austerity

A shared piece of tiramisu
savored bite by luscious bite
offers the same opportunity
for enlightenment as a
bare and austere life.

If pleasure focuses awareness,
and awareness opens to
the near embrace of now,
if the present moment grows
into gratitude and love,

then praise be to flour,
sugar, and cream, to the
divine energy that arises
from nothing and nowhere
to enliven every crumb
of this creation.

Drop of Nectar

At the tip of the
hummingbird's long beak,
a drop of nectar sits.
Before the bird flicks it off,
the perfect sphere shimmers
like a portal to a different world.
Isn't everything, closely noticed,
a doorway to another realm?
This ordinary morning has
its mystical counterpart and twin.
All it takes to be invited in
is the choice to see past the
surface tension to the ever-
changing unity beneath.

When Joy is Ripe for Reaping

The psalmist says, "Those who
sow in tears shall reap in joy."
If these words be true,
our destiny is surely joyful,
considering all the tears,
all the years of suffering
and doubt. If these words
be true, why not proclaim the
harvest feast, the day when joy
is ripe for reaping and
contentment is complete.

This is what I have to say to you. Enter the center of your being. Stand in the source of all inquiry, knowing, and unknowing.

Reclaim your wholeness by being the body and all its changing sensations. Receive the message of your emotions without believing they're the only show in town. Be the subtle energy that ebbs and flows, that brings healing and connection. Be the mind, witnessing thoughts, sinking into insight and unleashed creativity. Be the innate bliss and joy that arises when no part of you is exiled or left to fester in darkness.

At the center, be the conscious self without borders or limits. Slip outside personal identity to find that the infinite reality of truth has always been you. From the center of the center, let what you are express freely on all levels. Present, awake, and grateful for this moment, just be, without qualifiers or boundaries, and in the being, be at peace.

Just By Breathing

With each breath,
I take it in,
all the unique
outpourings of spirit
and the eloquent
expressiveness of now.

With each breath,
I let it out, all my
disempowerment
and doubt, my arms-
length distance from
the infinite and real.

Just by breathing,
I am healed.

Singularity and Oneness

In the intimacy between
the woodpecker's beak
and the tree trunk, I hear
singularity and oneness,
both at once. In the
wet splash of tear on
cheek, in the burble of
creek leaping over rocks
to run downstream, in the
silent energy that flows
from your eyes to my eyes
and back, I find the
source of mystery and love.

Look anywhere, listen with
focus in any moment,
turn inward to receive
the truth, and there is
always the vast and holy
field of knowing and
unknowing and the
particular one who
notices and takes it in.
This paradox of both/and
stretches past the edge of
mind to something much
less linear. The expansive
dance with All That Is
never ceases to leave me
speechless and amazed.

Healing Journey

Go gently into this good day,
appreciating the play
of opposites, the way
sunlight chases frost crystals
off the grass blades
as dawn melts into morning.

Take the one step you
can take right now,
open to whatever comes,
whether it meets your
expectations or shatters
them into a thousand
sparkling shards.

Go gently into this good day,
faith rising to the occasion,
fear receding just enough
to reveal the next step
on your healing journey.

Crucible of Truth

Just as I am, Lord,
let your love pour in.
Just as this day is,
let your miracles be
visible to me.
May I give myself
fully to your crucible
of truth and may my
heart open wide to
your presence inside,
outside, obvious, or
hidden, all of life a
pilgrimage with no
goal but to know you
so intimately that none
of your magnificence
is lost to me and none
of my longing
goes unanswered.

Joy to the World

Joy is the word
I receive when I
open my being and
let awareness lead.
One word, resplendent
in its simplicity,
like a star atop the tree.

Awakened and free,
joy dances through me,
takes my hand, spins me
round 'til I grow dizzy.
Joy points at my heart
and grins, points at my
head and nods, traces a
circle with one arm,
making sure the whole
of me is inside its
wide circumference,
and then gestures to
include the earth and sky.

Joy is everywhere.
No exceptions. None.
One word for the world
to live by is enough.

Updraft

Vulture in an updraft
has no need to flap
its wings. I try to learn
this easy lesson and
ride life's currents,
the warm air bearing
me up until my
problems seem as
nothing, far beneath
my outstretched wings.

Love Life

Love life—the sheer adventure
of sailing into the unknown.
I'm not speaking here only
of the bone and flesh life,
the visible and material.
Love the inner life too,
the life of spirit, joy, and
wisdom. Fully inhabit this
temple of the body, yes—
and also claim the mystery
of the unmanifest, the two
together weaving a seamless
whole that clothes you in light.

Love *this* life, not some imaginary
future when all your problems
have been solved, all your rough
edges sanded smooth.
Love *this* life with its impossible
demands. Open to its many gifts,
investigating whether what seem
like boundaries are really there
at all. Maybe your true nature
is vast beyond measure and the
opportunity to know yourself
inside and out is worth more
than any treasure.

One Brief Meditation

An ocean opens between
one thought and the next.
I fall in, swim, dive,
lose myself, and rise to the
surface where the mind
still compares, judges,
and tries to figure things out.

This silent sea of energy
and truth includes the visible
universe and the invisible too.
It's all here inside me,
the bodymind and the
unchanging field in which
the world arises.

My identity dissolves and
re-forms a dozen times
in one brief meditation.

Your Moment

The moment is here,
the moment you step
forward from fear
into light, the moment
that your soul takes flight.

Burrow no more in darkness
and despair. Dare to show
your radiant self,
the miracle of awakened
energy giving you wings
and the courage to be
human and divine
at the same time.

With this breath, you are
initiated into the depths
of freedom and love,
into the peril and perfection
of the moment as it truly is,
and you are right with it,
open, refusing to close down
or cower no matter what
challenges find you inside
or outside. This is your
moment to shine.

Tiger of Your Soul

Do not try to tame
the tiger of your soul
that paces inside its
cage of bones.
Its bold longing
to be free will lead
you past the weary
trudge of daily duties
and security. When the
tiger's eyes find yours,
do not break and run,
but welcome the
infusion of truth,
the unblinking gaze
that won't take no or
maybe as an answer.

This is what I have to say to you. Breathe in divinity, joy, love, silence, vastness, or contentment. Choose one, and you get all the others, too. Effortless inclusion. Spontaneous expansion. Breathe in joy and every quality you ascribe to divinity streams in to keep joy company. Breathe out joy and the great overflow of energy and grace goes with it, beginning to empty the closets, basement, and attic of the psyche.

You cannot breathe in joy and breathe out joy and avoid the shadows inside. Whatever arises, acknowledge, respect, and ultimately let it go. That's the path to being a spacious, open vehicle for light. That's the best way to be in dialogue with the divine. Joy informing joy. Joy including every emotion from grief to rage. Joy opening the floodgates of creation and being swept away by the ocean that is God.

Breathe in joy and breathe out joy and all that is holy, which is to say, all that is, will be yours in this instant of wholeness.

Ten Pieces of Advice for a Poet

1.   Listen within and do what you are told.

2.   Be willing to spin gold from straw and
     straw from absolutely nothing.

3.   Emulate the rabbit who somehow
     finds the only patch of grass not
     covered by deep snow.

4.   Let your love affair with words lead you
     into places you would never go alone.

5.   Take risks and try new things, knowing
     that most poems are stillborn, but the
     ones that live can rock your world.

6.   Sometimes sound and rhyme lead,
     and sometimes meaning; only you can
     choose to follow a fledgling poem into
     the unknown.

7.   Slow down enough to notice how the
     woodpecker's tail fans out when it tries
     to crack a seed.

8.   Write from love, not need.

9. Grow reasonably comfortable with fear, joy, anger, greed, shadows, sunlight, and the soul's insistence on screaming until you take it seriously.

10. Be unfailingly grateful for what you receive – diamond or coal dust, masterpiece or ash – all deserve to be equally appreciated.

Wildflowers

Meadow of miracles,
I am bewitched
by your surprises.
It isn't just the
daisies and bachelor
buttons, not just the
butterflies and finches,
but the whole array
of enchantments
reaching out to greet
me all at once,
clouds, honeybees,
and groundhogs – this is
landscape architecture
on the grandest scale,
creation and creator
dancing in the mid-day
heat. Monet might catch
this magic on canvas,
but I am content to let
my senses revel
in the moment,
life's kaleidoscope
turning, turning,
colors and shapes
waking up the joy
in me that recognizes
when it's time to stand
still and simply breathe.

Begin Again

I feel like a fraud,
all those poems out there
that speak of connection
and wholeness, when
for weeks, I've felt only
separate and fragmented.

I catch a glimpse of my
vast self, the truth that
isn't rattled by circumstance,
but it passes in a flash
to leave me stewing in
the juice of my despair.

I pray for the patience
to stay still, to let the
waves of feeling build
until they crash through
my defenses and I am
left spent, yet refreshed,
and ready to begin again.

Trust

When problems abound,
trust that solutions are
rising up to meet you from
the very ground of being.

When needs are great,
trust the abundance of the
universe to fill you in
surprising ways.

When darkness seems
impenetrable, trust light
to shine, the way made
plain one small step
at a time.

This Moment of Yoga

Breath by conscious breath,
I plumb the depths.
Awareness peels back each
layer, revealing the one
beneath until I come to rest.

Perhaps more layers remain,
or maybe I've reached the
center – it doesn't seem
to matter. All I know
is that stillness fills me.

My mind grows quiet
and for a few breaths
there is no next, no context,
no practice to perfect.
There is only this moment
of yoga.

Where I Am Right Now

A train whistle floats
like a dust mote in the quiet.
It is an enticing sound,
conjuring images of travel,
adventure, a footloose life,
as if I'm somehow bound,
as if freedom isn't already
my reality, as if steel rails
lead to a more desirable
experience than where
I am right now.

Blessing

May grace abound,
and ecstasy too. In the
fray of everyday life,
may you embody
your true nature.
May you breathe in
love and breathe out
love until love is your
only reality, even in
the midst of challenge.
May you not deny
difficulties or the
shadow side of life,
but find divine Presence
inside even the hardest
times. May miracles
come your way often –
and especially today.
Amen.

Sparrow at Sunrise

If vastness had a voice,
it wouldn't find fault.
Perhaps it would say,
in a slow and
deliberate way,
"It's all holy,"
Or maybe, like a
sparrow at sunrise,
it would let song be
its offering, the simple
trill of notes repeated
over and over, more
eloquent than any speech.

This is what I have to say to you. There are many responses you can have to any moment. Why not choose joy? Why not let divinity in to fill your cup with invisible gifts? What spills over into the world as joy is your most holy offering.

Joy says oneness is inevitable. Joy says raise your eyes to the broad blue sky or the heavy clouds weeping rain, and either way give thanks for air to breathe and people to love, for creatures to marvel at and for the moment, just as it is.

Joy says be your whole self, your natural self, your made-in-the-image-and-likeness-of-God self. However you are drawn to express, be it prayer, movement, stillness, writing, song, or silence, allow that expression to be full and flowing, moving from the formless into form and expanding your awareness all the while.

Joy says it's a great day to be alive because you are. Isn't life itself miracle enough to bow before in awe? When joy tickles your innards, let your giggles lighten the load on your shoulders until you can lay that weight down and walk away, a new, unburdened being.

Acknowledgements

First and foremost, I thank my husband Richard Faulds, who shares my life journey with such love, humor, and honesty. When I get lost, he reminds me of the truth. And when I started putting together yet another poetry book, his enthusiasm and stellar editorial skills brought the best out of me and my writing. This book is in your hands in large part because of Richard's belief in it and me.

Thank you to all the people who helped out on the Virginia home-front over the last year: Rita and Paul Milelli, Sneha Karen Jegart, Roberta Hamlin, Margaret Klapperich, Pat Ward, and my colleagues at the Woodrow Wilson Presidential Library: Peggy Dillard, Jacque Frankfort, and Connie Murray.

Gratitude to Amanda LoRusso whose blithe spirit and disarming boldness always made me smile. Don't settle for anything less than a remarkable life!

So many friends helped make this past year at Kripalu a positive one: Marcy and Bruce Balter, Heather Bilotta, Michael Bower, Tara Brach, Raya Buckley, Larissa Hall Carlson, Yoganand Michael Carroll, Dorothy Cochrane, Stephen Cope, Bettina Dudley, Ted Fernald, Moose Foran, Kristin Forester, Jonathan Foust, Ann Greene, Bonny and Dink Griffin, Joel and Tora Huntington, Myron Katz, Tara Knicos, Kathy Kuser, Nancy Macy, Vandita Kate Marchesiello, Susanlee Mascaro, Richard Miller, Justin and Adele Morreale, Laura Mushenko, Ed Nardi, Roxie Newberry, Todd Norian, Lisa Pletzer, Christina Polizzo, Lynne Pouliot, Nadia Puttini, Anne Romans, Erich Schiffmann, Anna Taneburgo, Peter,

Sachi, and Yatri Taussig, Marc Paul Volavka, Kevin Wason, Carole Weinstein, Tresca Weinstein, Paul Weiss, and all of the people I've interacted with at Kripalu – trustees, guests, volunteers, and staff, who together create a sangha that supports, uplifts, and inspires.

I thank David Lipsius for being a true yogi willing to take on the task of leading Kripalu back to its roots and forward into the next stage of its evolution as a yoga center and spiritual community. Thanks as well to all the other managers and staff who help to create the safe and sacred space at Kripalu.

I thank my sister Marianne Spitzform for being one courageous woman and for supporting me from afar in significant ways. Big thanks to my brother Peter Spitzform and his wife Rose O'Connell for their huge hearts and their commitment to making this a more just and equitable world. To my in-laws, John and Kay Faulds, I acknowledge your unfailing love and support.

In memory of Jack Glasser, Kripalu's dining room greeter extraordinaire, I smile every single time I walk through the doors for a meal.

Profound gratitude to yoga teachers everywhere, and especially the members of the Kripalu Yoga Teachers Association who share my poetry with their students. Without you and your support, this book and a precious facet of my life work would not exist.

And to everyone else who lent a hand, or heart, or helpful act, please accept my nameless but sincere appreciation.

Index of Titles and First Lines

Danna can be reached by e-mail at
yogapoems@aol.com